YOUR JOURNEY INTO REAL ESTATE INVESTING

The Beginner's Guide to Getting Started

Russell Lowder

Introduction

As you work your way through this book, I wish you the best of understanding and I hope this book will make your journey into real estate investing easy.

What is real estate?

Real estate may be a term used to describe tangible property, like land, structures, air rights over the land, and subsurface rights under the land. "Realty" may be a phrase utilized in business to explain the creation, acquisition, and sale of real estate.

Due to its importance as an engine of economic expansion, reality affects the American economy. It should be seen as an investment or simply a sale made to satisfy the needs of the customer or business for both individuals and corporations.

Real estate, which is commonly cited as "real property," is technically land along with the other observable improvements that might be put in or rest upon it. Because of the enhancement, a road or a structure may be constructed. A septic system, for instance, is an example of anything that has been placed into the world.

Numerous factors are involved in reality. It's a transitional area between unimproved and improved. It should either be bought or sold. It's going to be owned by the government, a business, or a private individual. The economy is also directly impacted by certain factors, like the continuing development of land and the people or organizations that allow ownership transfers.

Here is a summary of the steps you need to take to become a real estate investor.

Acquire real estate knowledge.
The first step in determining the best approach to managing your assets as a new investor is to get familiar with the fundamentals of real estate. To understand the ins and outs of the real estate business, think about enrolling in a few real estate courses. This may position you to identify the best investment prospects and prevent squandering cash on unpromising ventures.

Make a business strategy.
Creating a real estate investing plan may assist you in making smart financial decisions.

Know what kind of investments you want to make, how much working capital you have, and what your expected return is. Decide on any high-risk investments you want to make, and then plan your budget appropriately. Determine if you want to approach your real estate plan actively or passively. To determine where your money might be best used for your sort of investment, speak with an adviser if required.

Research the local market.

Pay close attention to home market predictions and keep up with any recent developments in home market investing news. If you're investing in residential real estate, study the burgeoning communities, the properties that are available for sale, and the properties that aren't selling. Pay attention to what, where, and when tenants are renting. When making an investment in commercial real estate, such as shops or residential apartment complexes, take the neighborhood demographics and the area's foot traffic into account. Keep up with the most recent real estate development laws and rules, including zoning, property taxes, and availability.

Speak to other investors.
You may learn the best practices for your real estate investment plan by networking with other seasoned investors. Successful investors may be able to provide you with helpful advice for managing real estate or making investments in buildings. They may also provide insightful guidance on how to diversify your real estate holdings. Additionally, you may come across some possible collaborators for future investment projects.

Consider passive real estate investing.
Similar to investing in the stock market, there are numerous possibilities in real estate where you may buy a piece of a pool of assets and see your equity increase in value. Companies that own and manage real estate are referred to as real estate investment trusts (REITs), and if they are publicly listed,

ordinary people may invest in them for passive income. Another way for investors to participate in a collection of real estate ventures with promising futures is via real estate mutual funds. Rich businesspeople may sometimes use crowdsourcing to finance some real estate investments while contracting others to handle the properties' logistical needs.

10 Good Reasons to Take a Position in Real Estate

Real estate investment may add plenty of cash to your checking account, but it also has potential risks and requires study. Here are some of the most significant justifications for land investment in the world.

Consistent cash flow

Real estate ownership might increase your monthly income. If you invest in residential or commercial property, you will rent out your space to renters. Rent payments will thereafter be sent to you every month. Just be careful: If you would like to reduce the likelihood that your renters may someday quit paying their rent, you'll have to look at their payment histories.

Excessive Profit

You may be able to sell the important estate you own for a healthy profit if its value rises over time. But keep in mind: recognition isn't a given. To achieve such high profits, you want to invest in the correct real estate market.

Stability Over Time

Real estate could also be held for a variety of years while you expect it to be understood since it's a long-term investment. While you wait for your property's value to increase, you will also make a monthly income by renting out your property.

Tax Benefits

Real estate investing has tax advantages. Your property taxes, mortgage interest, property management fees, property insurance, the price of ongoing maintenance, the value of repairs, and the money you spend advertising your property to potential renters are just some of the costs associated with owning an investment property that can be written off. The gain you create if you sell your property for more than you paid for it won't be subject to revenue enhancement. Instead, it'll be subject to capital gains tax, which has generally lower tax rates than revenue enhancement. Even fewer capital gains taxes are going to be due if you invest in communities called opportunity zones.

The utilization of a variety

Your financial diversification is increased once you include land, which helps shield you from market fluctuations. For example, a downturn within the economy is causing some equities to suffer. Your portfolio of investment properties should still be rising in value, shielding you from the losses your other assets are suffering.

Residual Income

You needn't work daily to get the much-desired passive income that investment properties provide. Imagine you own a single-family or multifamily property and charge rent. Monthly rent payments are an example of passive income.

Capacity for Financial Leverage

You possibly haven't got the money to get homes outright when investing in land. Considering that you just want to rent a single-family house, the value could also be as high as $200,000. Leverage plays a role in this. Real leverage refers to the act of shopping for properties with the help of other people's funds. In this scenario, you'd borrow money from banks, mortgage companies, or credit unions and gradually pay it back. By doing this, you will increase the amount of real estate you possess without having to pay the entire price to try to do so.

Resistance to inflation

Realty investments are seen as inflation hedges. Home values and rental income often rise together with product and repair costs. Therefore, investment homes may provide you with increasing monthly income and appreciation to help safeguard your finances while the value of everything else rises.

Capitalization is a possibility

Increasing your cash, sometimes cited as building capital, could be a major objective of asset investment. You'll increase your capital once you sell a property whose value has increased. Investing in the correct properties that may increase in value is the key.

Satisfaction and Control

Other advantages that are not financial include owning investment homes. Owning an investment property enables you to be your own boss, which many investors find rewarding. Providing rental housing or attracting companies to commercial sites that will provide much-needed services to local communities are other ways you'll make a difference in your neighborhood.

The Difficulties of Asset Investing

Real estate investment has the potential for large returns, but it also carries significant risks and problems.

Liquidity

Property investments don't seem to be liquid. Once you've invested your money in a single-family residence, a dwelling, or a few business assets, you'll have to sell that property or the fraction you own to recover your investment. Bonds and equities are among the foremost assets. Selling stocks to access your money is straightforward.

Starting Money

You'll also need extra money to start investing in assets. Commercial and residential land is expensive. You'll have to apply for mortgage financing for these homes. Mutual funds, certificates of deposit, and stock investments often need much less initial cash.

Time

When investing in property, the returns often take time to materialize. Yes, you will charge rent to renters in either business or residential spaces. But often, these payments are simple enough to hide your mortgage or other maintenance expenses for an investment property. Once you sell the property over to procure it, you'll make lots of cash. However, you regularly have to wait a variety of years for the value of your properties to rise before you achieve that objective.

Location

When investing in property, location is everything. If your house isn't situated in a neighborhood where real estate values are rising, it generally won't increase in value. This suggests that finding the best investment property within the ideal location will need extensive investigation.

Advanced Real Estate Investing Tips

Although practically anybody may invest in real estate, specific traits distinguish some investors from others.

Nobody is an expert when it comes to real estate investment. Because of this, savvy real estate investors continue to learn throughout their lives. They understand when to ask for help.

To help you get the most out of your real estate investment plan, here are the top 10 professional recommendations for spending your money on Denver real estate.

When investing in real estate, pay attention to emerging regions.
One of the best real estate investment tips is to invest in newer communities. So, research to find areas with the biggest development prospects as well as enticing tax breaks for investment.

This will enable you to get a larger ROI in the long run.

Consider a property management company.
Another piece of professional real estate advice is to think about employing a property management firm to assist you with some of the routine responsibilities.

You may promote your rental properties, collect rent, screen tenants, handle property accounting, and arrange for rental inspections with the help of a competent property management firm. An alternative is to figure the rental value.

Investing in Different Real Estate Types.
You should also diversify your investment portfolio. In other words, it's not a good idea to store all of your investment properties in one place. You should do extensive research and invest in numerous communities.

Exercise caution while doing renovations.
Before renting out your rental properties, you'll want to make sure they're in top shape, but this doesn't imply going overboard. Even though granite countertops are great, can you afford them? Create a prudent budget and stick to it.

Keep a cash reserve on hand.
If you decide to invest in real estate, you should have an emergency fund. Landlords need to budget for unanticipated expenses. A

simple problem might become a large one if you lack the funds.

Be aware of openings.

Some investors base their real estate assessments solely on projected cash flow. However, you should also consider open positions. There will always be openings. Be mindful of this while looking for houses to purchase.

Gain an understanding of tax laws.

One of the most important pieces of real estate advice for landlords is to educate themselves on the applicable tax regulations. It's a good idea to understand Schedule E (Form 1040). But you also need to know which tax deductions are appropriate.

To Avoid Excessive Spending.

You should base your real estate investment decisions more on study than on instinct.

Before renting out houses to Denver renters that are contemplating their property leasing alternatives, do your homework and determine how much you need to spend on repairs and upkeep.

If the numbers just don't add up, wait until you come across better opportunities.

Continue learning

As was previously discussed, if you want to succeed as a real estate investor, you'll need to continue learning new things. Keep up with the latest legislation, fashions, and rules. By doing this, you'll have a competitive edge that will benefit you.

Work with a CPA

You may want to think about employing an accountant if your real estate portfolio expands and your obligations rise. This expert will be knowledgeable about tax rules and may greatly increase your savings. A wise investment was made.

How to think like a real estate investor

One adage that might mask a myriad of issues for an investor is "buy cheap, sell high." The advice is far from obvious, particularly if one is interested in real estate as an investment, even if the words themselves appear easy to grasp and put into practice. In conclusion, real estate investment may be a challenging industry for beginners.

However, for individuals who possess the ability to "think like a real estate investor," the opportunities and rewards are almost limitless. Take some time to comprehend the real estate investing process rather than adopting a short, simplistic statement like the one above. To assist you in getting started, consider the following ideas:

Recognize the Contract and Your Role

Do not skimp on your comprehension of the agreement and your obligations therein. You may ensure that your worries are addressed by asking pertinent questions and ensuring that you are well informed about the data. To fully comprehend the project, request any recent pictures, blueprints, or drawings of the site. These inquiries shouldn't come as a surprise to the borrower. If so, look for a different bargain.

Holding out for the best bargain

Trying to budge on any point in negotiations may quickly backfire.You must have the ability to think like the borrower and comprehend that without certain conditions being met, the loan is useless to them. Everyone's time and effort are wasted when you act as if your wants are the only ones that need to be addressed.

Get the Proper Security

The fact that the loan is secured by real estate is one of the main advantages of a real estate transaction. Once you are aware of this, you may use the loan-to-value (LTV) ratio to your advantage to push the transaction closer to your "comfort zone."

An Excellent Place to Begin

While having competent counsel is helpful, grasping these concepts is the first step toward thinking like a real estate investor. Private money lenders are masters at matching reliable borrowers with capable investors, and they can explain everything to everyone, from the fundamentals to intricate intricacies. They know how to think like a real estate investor since they are so closely connected to the sector.

This book's objective is simple: to provide you with the big and wide picture of how real estate investment works and give you the fundamental skills to go beyond the all-important issue of how to get started.

I've thus included a list of topics in the book.

Chapter 1

Common Real Estate Questions New Investors Ask

15 Frequently Asked Real Estate Questions by New Investors

Beginners may find real estate investing intimidating due to its breadth. Many new investors fail because they enter the business without adequate planning and knowledge. But successful people frequently develop the practice of posing real estate-related queries.

When you first start, it is practically impossible to know everything there is to know about real estate investing. However, by asking questions, you can gain knowledge from those who have experience and become more familiar with current trends. Additionally, you'll be able to steer clear of pricey mistakes that are avoidable.

Some real estate-related queries are asked more frequently than others. Therefore, it is a good idea to become familiar with the responses to these questions before you plunge into the world of real estate investing. Here are 15 questions prospective investors frequently have about real estate.

1. How do I calculate the value of a rental property?
The majority of new investors looking to purchase an investment property refer to our real estate FAQ. There are several ways to

estimate the value of a piece of real estate. Comparative market analysis, on the other hand, is the most typical technique for figuring out how much a property is worth. This is a thorough analysis of recently sold comparable properties in the same neighborhood. You may obtain real estate comps with Mashvisor's investment property calculator.

2. What real estate investing plan is best for me?
This is another typical real estate question that novice investors have before entering the market. There are numerous opportunities for investing in real estate. As a result, many novice real estate investors frequently struggle to decide which method to employ. Your willingness to commit time and money will determine the ideal real estate investing approach for you. It's crucial to take into

account your long-term objectives for real estate investing.

3. Where can I locate a decent investment property?
If you want to be successful in real estate investing, you must understand how to find lucrative investment properties. You must conduct a thorough analysis of the city, area, and investment property to achieve this. However, this procedure is somewhat laborious and complicated. To identify successful investment properties across the US, you can use Mashvisor's real estate tools to rapidly and reliably do real estate market analysis and investment property analysis.

4. Can I start buying real estate without any money?
Financing for investment properties comes in a variety of forms. But not everyone can get a conventional mortgage because you need to

have a big enough down payment and meet additional criteria. You will need to be more inventive if you can't pay cash for the property or don't have enough cash for a down payment. New real estate investors can start in several ways with little or no money down. Here are some tactics to think about:

- Real estate joint ventures
- Private or hard money loans.
- Purchaser finance
- Wholesaling
- home equity loans

5. If I already own a home, will real estate investing be simpler?
If you already own a home, you can invest in real estate more easily as a novice. This might be your home or another investment property. You can borrow more on an existing property and amass a sizable real estate investment portfolio much more

quickly. But ultimately, it will depend on your financial circumstances and investment objectives.

6. Will I require a real estate agent while purchasing a home?

You may invest on your own in a rental property. However, if you are new to real estate investing, it is highly advised that you deal with a real estate agent. The procedure can be quite demanding and time-consuming without an agent. An agent will guide you through every step of the purchasing process and make sure you adhere to all regulations. They will enable you to research markets, get pre-approved for a loan, find an attorney, negotiate a transaction, close a deal, and much more. But be sure to thoroughly interview potential agents before selecting one that is knowledgeable and a good fit for you.

7. Where can I find information on real estate investing?
Successful real estate investing depends on real estate education. You must be knowledgeable about a variety of topics, including searching for and analyzing properties; finance; tenant screening; etc. This does not, however, imply that you must attend college to learn about real estate investing. You can learn more about real estate fundamentals from a variety of other sources, both free and paid. Because of technology, anyone may now get information about real estate investing. These sources include, among others, books, podcasts, blogs, and newspapers.

8. Could I perhaps buy real estate outside of my home state?
As a novice real estate investor, you need to think about acquiring an investment house nearby. If the property is accessible by car,

dealing with your service providers and renters will be simpler. It is best to wait until you have adequate expertise before investing in a property out of state. Having said that, there are situations when purchasing a house outside of your state may be more advantageous. For instance, you may discover that residences elsewhere in the US are more lucrative or more reasonably priced than those in your neighborhood. You should do in-depth market research and carefully consider your alternatives before deciding where to invest in real estate.

9. How will I choose the amount of rent I should charge for my home?
Every investor should be able to answer this crucial real estate question before placing an ad for their rental property. A property's rental potential is crucial. If overestimated, the house can sit empty for a very long time. Negative cash flow might occur if it is set too

low. You must seek similar homes (rental comps) in the neighborhood and check what they are being listed for to get a reasonable estimate of the monthly rental value. The state of the local market should also be taken into account.

10. How do I choose the ideal renter for my rental home?
Your business's performance will be impacted by the caliber of your tenants. The ideal renter maintains the rental home and pays rent on time. You should do careful tenant screening if you want to find a suitable renter. Make sure you verify their identification and look into their credit and rent payment history.

11. Who covers the utility bills?
Renters are typically responsible for paying utilities such as electricity, gas, water, and telephone unless all costs are included in the

rent. To prevent any misunderstandings in the future, the landlord must make this clear in the leasing agreement.

12. What happens if the renter damages my property?

Possibly the most frequent concern of landlords is this. Consequently, it is one of the most frequently asked real estate questions. When the renter moves in, the landlord should request a security deposit to lessen the possibility of property damage. The security deposit will cover any damage and serve as a reminder to the renter to leave the property in the same condition that they found it. When the lease expires, the cost of correcting any damage that was not paid for by the tenant when it happened will be taken out of the security deposit. However, reasonable wear and tear should be allowed for by the landlord.

13. What happens if the renter declines to pay the rent?
You may give the renter notice to vacate the rental property if they refuse to pay. The court may be asked for any unpaid rent. You may protect yourself against nonpayment of rent by purchasing rent assurance insurance as a precaution. If the renter is unable to pay the rent for whatever reason, the insurance company will cover the rent for a certain number of months. Upon submission of your application, you will get a policy paper outlining the rules and regulations you must follow.

14. Should I make any improvements before renting out my investment home?
If your property is in excellent shape, renting it out is always a smart idea. Renting a clean, well-painted, and outfitted rental home will rent more quickly and for a higher price. However, you shouldn't overspend on home

improvements. Only invest in upgrades that will raise the property's value without being too expensive.

15. When will I get my return?

Most novice real estate investors who have such inquiries are often trying to find a fast method to become wealthy. Real estate investment may be a successful venture. The majority of the time, however, it won't make you wealthy overnight or even in a matter of months. Before seeing significant results, you will need to put in a lot of effort and be patient. Your results will also vary based on your plan and the state of the market.

Chapter 2

Real Estate Investment Niches

An Explanation Of A Real Estate Niche

The real estate market is enormous and extremely varied. There are various types of properties, each with its own operating characteristics, risk/return profile, and amount of management obligations.For instance, maintaining a 150,000 SF commercial shopping complex is considerably different than managing a single-family house. Due to the size and diversity of the industry, investors frequently focus on "niches," which are discrete regions within a much larger market.

Ten Different Commercial Real Estate Specialties Are Listed Below For Potential Investors To Think About

1. Commercial

A piece of property that is bought and leased to businesses to make money through rental revenue, price appreciation, or both is referred to as commercial real estate. There are four categories of properties that are commonly used in commercial real estate.

- Retail

Direct-to-consumer retail firms are housed in retail investment sites. Strip malls, regional malls, power centers, and the grocery store-anchored centers that we invest in are typical examples of retail properties. Retail assets appeal to investors because of their long lease terms, excellent locations, and great visibility. Many reputable investment companies, like ours, work with private buyers to buy and manage them.

- Office

The space required for businesses to run daily is located in office leasing facilities. Office buildings can be used for anything from typical office purposes like an accountancy firm to more specialized ones like research labs or medical offices. Office buildings are popular with investors due to their long lease terms and prime locations, and they can acquire access to them by working with a reputable firm.

- Industrial

Manufacturing, distribution, and storage of goods are all done on industrial premises. They consist of storage facilities, logistical hubs, and small industrial facilities. Due to their minimal running expenses and economic necessity, investors favor them. Once more, you can buy them directly or in conjunction with an experienced real estate company.

- Self-Storage

Personal belongings are kept in self-storage buildings for people. They are frequently built with a variety of unit sizes and situated in suburban areas where land is less expensive. Because of their high development potential and minimal operating expenses, investors favor self-storage.

Direct purchases of commercial real estate are possible, but the best choice for most individual investors is probably to partner with a seasoned real estate company like a private equity firm or real estate investment trust (REIT) and buy a fractional share.

2. Duplexes, triplexes, and duplexes
A duplex (2 units), triplex (3 units), or quadplex (4 units) may be a fantastic choice for investors who prefer residential real estate but want a greater size than just a single-family house. Investors choose these properties because they are far less expensive than commercial assets, have fewer onerous property management requirements, and typically have more favorable lending terms.

3. Apartment buildings and multifamily housing developments

A multifamily complex or commercial apartment building is one with more than four units. These types of properties can be found in almost all cities and have various layouts. For instance, garden-style, multi-building properties are frequently found in suburban locations where there is more accessible land, but high-rise apartment complexes are frequently found in the downtown districts of major cities (like New York City).

Multifamily properties appeal to investors because of their steady, reliable cash flows; good loan terms; high occupancy rates; and renters who prioritize their mortgage payments in hard times.

4. Hospitality

All types of hotels and motels are regarded as hospitality properties, regardless of their cost or degree of service. These short-term rentals, which normally last from one night to a week or ten days, can be very profitable as long as they are filled. Investors like hospitality assets because of their high visibility and high rental prices.

5. Individually Detached Family

A single-family detached home makes the most sense as a starting point for real estate investors. It might be used as an Airbnb, a vacation rental, or a monthly rental for a single individual or a small family. Single-family homes are a favorite among investors due to their relative affordability, wide availability of financing, low-interest rates, and steady rent payments.

6. Condos

Condominiums are a popular initial investment for new investors. They have many characteristics in common with single-family houses and townhomes, but their key differences are that they are attached to other units; they are a part of a larger building; and the monthly payment likely includes HOA dues, which can increase the carrying cost. Similar to why single-family houses are preferred by investors, condos are preferred for their relative affordability, ease of access to financing, and plenty of rental opportunities.

7. People in groups

A variety of investment property options fall under the category of residential communities, including retail, multifamily, townhomes, single-family homes, and special-use situations like golf courses. These properties are preferred by investors because they include the components of a successful investing strategy. For instance, membership or age (let's say 55+ years old) restrictions are routinely used to limit access to communities. For instance, a businessman might purchase a luxurious home in a community with a golf course, a shopping center, and a fitness facility. These extra comforts can increase interest in the home, which might lead to steady increases in market value.

8. Land

For someone with a long-term view, land might be a good investment because it can be used for a variety of purposes. For example, it might be used as farmland to grow crops. Or it might develop into one of the aforementioned types. In the right location, land can appreciate quickly and be sold to a real estate developer for a profit. Investors are drawn to land because of the depreciation it produces and the variety of applications it can one day be put to.

9. Parking Resources

Parking facilities are regularly used to provide spaces for people to park in high-density locations like corporate districts and high-traffic areas like sports complexes, shopping malls, and airports. Due to their significant cash flow and minimal operating costs, parking structures are preferred by investors since they can be extremely profitable in the right location.

10. Health

Medical properties provide for the needs of medical tenants. They could be dental offices, medical centers, urgent care centers, or labs. Due to the continued demand for medical services, investors prefer medical offices since they generally have long-term leases and typically have tenants with lower credit risks.

Additional Niche Opportunities

Opportunities for real estate investing are not just available in the aforementioned markets. Depending on their level of knowledge, risk tolerance, and time horizon, other potential investment niches for investors include foreclosed or distressed assets; mobile homes; student housing; short sales; house flipping; rent to own; or specialty assets like golf courses or theme parks.

Chapter 3

Real Estate Investment Tactics

An excellent way to diversify an investment portfolio with a holding that produces returns equal to those of the stock market but with less volatility is to own real estate. Additionally, residential real estate offers investors certain tax advantages, and investors may employ leverage to increase their total profits.

There are several methods for investors to profit from real estate, even if directly owning investment properties is the most popular. Here are 10 real estate investment tactics that experienced and novice investors can both employ.

10 Techniques For Investing In Real Estate

Depending on your objectives and time frame, certain real estate investment tactics will perform better for you than others.

1. Purchase and hold property
Purchasing and keeping SFR properties is a real estate investment strategy intended to generate rental income, profit from long-term property value growth, and take advantage of certain tax advantages available to real estate investors.

For both novice and experienced investors, SFR property is undoubtedly the most well-liked real estate investment. According to the most recent U.S. Single-Family Rental Outlook study from Green Street, an independent real estate research and advisory business, SFRs comprise 35% of all rental properties in the nation.

SFRs could be quite simple to locate, acquire, and run. For residential real estate, there are several financing possibilities, ranging from traditional and government-backed loans to private and portfolio lenders.

In almost the last 20 years, the median sales price of homes sold in the U.S. has climbed by over 200%, yet the demand for rental housing is still high. Even so, the net income from rental property may vary as a result of upkeep, repairs, or prospective vacancies, and some investors may want a more passive approach to investing.

2. Put rental revenue to use.
Many buy-and-hold real estate investors adopt the complementary approach of reinvesting rental revenue.
The "snowball" technique preserves net cash flow from one rental property until funds are available for the down payment on a second rental property.

Then, until there is enough money for a third rental property, the net cash flow from both rental properties is preserved.

Similar to a snowball rolling down a hill, the amount of money earned grows as an investor's portfolio of rental properties expands.

Some owners reinvest rental revenue to pay off a mortgage on a piece of property more quickly; some make extra mortgage payments. The investor does a cash-out refinance to convert accumulated equity into cash so that they may buy another rental property once there is sufficient equity from combined appreciation and mortgage prepayments.

3. Housebreaking

The potential need for a sizable down payment is one disadvantage of investing in rental property. A real estate investment tactic called "house hacking" is utilized by homeowners who don't yet have enough cash to buy a rental home.

The rental of a spare bedroom or the conversion of a basement into a studio apartment are two instances of home hacking. Home rental property down payments are made through savings from home hacking rents until finances are available.

Some investors may also use a low-down-payment Federal Housing Administration (FHA) or Veterans Affairs (VA) loan to buy a modest, multifamily property. The requirement that the borrower reside in one of the units as their principal home is one of the possible disadvantages of this strategy. However, living next to renters is a great opportunity to learn about real estate investment and obtain practical property management expertise.

4. BRRRR

Real estate investors utilize the BRRRR method to acquire fixer-upper properties utilizing short-term financing, perform any necessary repairs, rent the properties to eligible tenants, and then refinance and withdraw cash after the properties have a stable history of positive cash flow.

In that an investor repeats the same action, the BRRRR real estate investment approach is comparable to the snowball effect. BRRRR is often a more advantageous option for an active investor who has the time and expertise to do tasks themselves or who has a reliable, cost-efficient network of handymen and contractors to assist with renovating.

Short-term financing often entails high loan fees and interest rates, so an investor must be cautious not to run out of money before the property starts to cash flow. This is one disadvantage of BRRRR.

5. Restoring and reselling

If everything goes according to plan, house flipping is a high-risk real estate investment technique with a potentially high payout.

Since they only want to retain a property for a short time, investors who repair and flip properties do not want to be landlords. A flipper may choose to hang onto an inexpensive property and hope to benefit from appreciation after finding and buying it. Alternatively, they may choose to undertake smart improvements to boost the value of the property.

Investors who are unable to flip a house fast or who misjudge the cost of renovations may run out of money. Fixing and flipping is best suited for people with substantial expertise in determining the fair market value of a house, the real cost of improvements, and enough funds to complete the project on schedule and under budget.

6. Real estate wholesale

A version of repairing and flipping, real estate wholesaling is an investment technique in which the property is never taken over by the wholesaler.

As an alternative, a real estate wholesaler looks for a distressed property with a motivated seller, contracts the house at a discount, determines the cost of repairs and the property's final fair market value, and then assigns the purchase and sale agreement to another investor in return for a small wholesale fee.

For real estate wholesaling to be effective, it takes a lot of effort, market expertise, and strong negotiation skills to persuade an owner to sell their property for less than the fair market value. In many jurisdictions, a distributor of real estate also has to have a license.

For those with little investment money, real estate wholesaling could be a smart investment plan. Some seasoned real estate wholesalers use "real estate bird dogs" to find distressed properties, who are then compensated with a tiny referral fee.

7. REIGs

Small funds called real estate investment groups (REIGs) acquire groupings of rental properties and then let investors purchase those properties from the group.

The REIG manages the marketing of unoccupied properties, tenant screening, rent collection, property management, and upkeep in return for a portion of the monthly rental revenue. When the properties in the group are sold, investors in a REIG

profit from their shares of any equity growth and recurrent rental revenue.

People searching for a hands-off real estate investment approach may find a REIG to be a viable alternative, but it's important to investigate management and their prior record of success or failure.

8. REITs

A variety of real estate assets, including residential build-to-rent (BTR) subdivisions, commercial real estate, or special-use buildings like data centers and cold storage facilities, are invested in by real estate investment trusts (REITs), which may be publicly or privately owned businesses.

At least 90% of REITs' income must be distributed as dividends to shareholders. They may be a useful strategy to diversify a portfolio of investments to make money from real estate without actually owning any real estate. Long-term leases with credit tenants are usual for investment-grade assets owned by a REIT. Publicly listed REITs are more liquid than other real estate investments because their shares may be purchased or sold on an exchange.

REITs, however, don't provide some of the benefits of directly owning a rental property, such as having direct control over choices about property management.

9. Crowdfunding

Online real estate investment platforms called crowdfunds allow investors to combine their cash to purchase shares of premium commercial and residential properties, including newly constructed homes, apartment complexes, and commercial real estate that has been stabilized.

Crowdfunding may be a great method to get exposure to properties that are out of reach

for the majority of investors. If a project is lucrative, crowdfund investors will get monthly pro-rata distributions of net income along with a portion of any profits.
Shares sometimes have lockup periods until a project is stable or during times of economic instability, which is one of the disadvantages of crowdfunding. To find lucrative prospects, finance and build the project, and lease and manage the property to increase asset value and cash flow, investors must also rely on the expertise of the crowdfund sponsor.

10. Individual lending
Instead of investing in stock, private lenders finance real estate loans. Private lenders give money to real estate investors searching for an alternative to conventional financing sources, such as house flippers, as opposed to buying the rental property themselves.

Private lenders generate income through lending fees and interest rates just as a typical bank does. But generally speaking, costs and interest rates are greater.

Even while private lending could be a wonderful strategy to earn consistent interest revenue, there is a chance that a borrower would fail and the lender would have to take back a partly refurbished home. Because of this, private lenders have real estate investment knowledge and know how to safeguard themselves if a property has to be repossessed.

Chapter 4

Ways to Find Incredible Real Estate Offers

The ability to locate excellent offers is one of the most important components of real estate investment. However, it might be difficult to locate decent offers in today's cutthroat marketplace. Good real estate opportunities won't simply come your way. Consequently, how can you create a competitive advantage?

Real estate investing is mostly a numbers game, and that is something you must grasp. You must examine several options to choose a nice property. Many investors make the fatal error of depending just on one method when looking for investment properties to buy. By using a range of efficient real estate lead generation tactics, the most successful real estate investors are those who can locate fantastic real estate opportunities before anybody else.

15 Ways to Find Real Estate Offers

1. Inform your social circle.
Informing everyone you know that you are purchasing real estate is one of the simplest and most efficient methods to locate bargains. Inform your friends, family, coworkers, and other people in your social circle.

Make it a practice to let people know that you are seeking real estate bargains. Even if they aren't trying to sell something, they could know someone who is. When a chance occurs, people will think of you first if they know you as someone who buys properties.

2. Establish connections with real estate experts.
By networking with other industry experts, you may potentially locate real estate bargains. Professionals with access to off-market real estate transactions are many. Local real estate agents, builders, mortgage brokers, property managers, real estate lawyers, lenders, wholesalers, and other property investors fall under this category. Anybody working in the real estate sector may provide quality leads.

Join neighborhood real estate investing groups, go to neighborhood gatherings, and let others know what you do. Your best source of fantastic offers will eventually be your real estate network. Networking is essential if you want to have a successful real estate investment career since real estate is a relationship-based industry.

3. Use the Multiple Listing Service to search (MLS)

The MLS is the most frequently used resource for finding investment property for sale. The homes that real estate agents are attempting to market for their customers are listed there. You must get assistance from a real estate agent who has access to the MLS since the MLS is not open to the general public.

The drawback of the conventional approach is the high level of competition and the likelihood of bidding wars. However, you may still discover fantastic real estate bargains this way if you work with a competent agent and have a pre-approval letter.

4. Consult an estate agent.
You may locate real estate bargains outside of the MLS with the aid of real estate agents. Agents that are knowledgeable about the neighborhood housing market will often be aware of off-market houses that are set to reach the market thanks to their network and expertise. Find a real estate agent that has expertise in investment properties.

5. Examine direct mail advertising.
Finding off-market bargains may also be accomplished via direct mail marketing. To use this tactic, you must notify homeowners through postcards or letters that you want to purchase their property. In actuality, some homeowners may not be considering selling their properties until they get an alluring offer. However, because you may not receive

a response immediately, this tactic calls for perseverance and patience.

6. Use social networking sites.
Social networking is one of the most effective ways to reach a large audience.By setting up and maintaining an active social media profile for your company, you might get worthwhile real estate transactions. Posting blogs and useful content to your feed often will increase your following.

7. Put the Driving for Dollars Plan into Action.
Driving for cash is one of the most affordable and tried-and-true tactics. Simply getting in your vehicle and driving around the communities you wish to invest in to look for distressed homes can help you uncover discounted houses. Watch out for unoccupied properties with deteriorating exteriors, such as peeling paint, overgrown grass, broken

windows, and missing shingles. These are some telltale signals that the owner is having trouble keeping the home up to date and could be under pressure to reduce the asking price.

Find out who owns the property by writing down the address, then get in touch with them to show your interest.

8. Examine property auctions.
Searching for auction homes is another approach to uncovering off-market properties that are selling for a bargain. Attending nearby real estate auctions may help you locate foreclosed and REO homes. Additionally, you may search a variety of online auction websites like Auction.com. The fact that these homes are being offered "as is" poses a risk, so bear that in mind. They need a lot of paperwork and often want monetary payments.

9. Examine public records.
Pre-foreclosures and short sales are often found in public records. Smart real estate investors will keep up with public records since they are aware that these properties might be profitable real estate acquisitions.

10. Check out Craigslist.
On Craigslist, look for nearby real estate that is for sale and consider contacting the owners. Regularly doing this will help you uncover possible bargains. To avoid paying real estate agent commissions, a lot of homeowners advertise their properties for sale on Craigslist.

11. Look for signs that say "For Sale by Owner."
People who wish to sell their homes for less might post FSBO signs in key locations like shopping malls and major crossroads. Such

homes may be a source of fantastic real estate bargains since they aren't often properly promoted and the sellers are frequently driven to sell.

12. Place an ad in a landlord's publication.
You might place an advertisement seeking real estate bargains in your area's landlord magazine or trade newspaper. You're more likely to locate a landlord who wants to sell their property if you target landlords.

13. Build a credible website.
Developing your website is a fantastic way to take advantage of digital real estate marketing in 2021. Your website should professionally display your work. It should also be well optimized for search engines.

14. Start a blog.
Content marketing is a fantastic technique to increase website traffic and lead generation. Think about writing frequent blogs that are informative for your neighborhood, especially for homeowners trying to sell. Don't forget to mention that you are purchasing real estate.

15. Use websites for real estate.
There are many real estate websites where you can do an internet search for properties. This real estate investing software makes it simple for investors to locate the greatest home offers in the US.

Every investor should have the ability to locate real estate offers. Most investors who exclusively use the MLS are unaware that the majority of real estate transactions never even appear on the MLS. Putting many marketing initiatives into action is the key to discovering fantastic real estate prospects. Keep in mind to always assess and enhance your marketing plans and tactics.

Chapter 5

Methods for Financing Your Real Estate Offers

There are hundreds of real estate financing choices available in today's financial industry. Most individuals find it impossible to operate entirely on cash, and investors know that spreading your wealth over many properties may result in a 50% or greater revenue return. As a result, even those who could go all-cash often chose not to, despite the increased risk.

Although traditional mortgages are still the most popular option, many real estate investors find them unattractive or impractical due to the 20% down payment and stringent financing restrictions. The security of all-cash deals and traditional mortgages' low-interest rates aren't always the best match for everyone due to their various drawbacks, but there are alternative real estate financing solutions that have their advantages, including these eight:

1. Owner Financing

You may avoid costly bank costs and pay the owner directly if you can locate a homeowner who owns his property entirely, wants to sell it, and is prepared to offer the financing. The transaction can be completed more quickly and easily, but you will probably have to pay a higher interest rate. Because most mortgages contain a due-on-sale provision that permits the mortgage holder to foreclose on the property right away should the owner sell it, the seller cannot retain a mortgage on the property with owner financing. Some investors take the chance that the bank won't agree to this, but the majority demand that the owner be the only owner.

2. Home equity loan

It is sometimes simpler to get a home equity loan using existing property rather than applying for a brand-new loan if you already have equity in a particular piece of real estate. If you have enough equity built up, banks may often accept this in the form of a loan (HEIL) or a line of credit (HELOC). The bank will only lend up to a particular amount, often 90% of the entire worth of your current home, less any outstanding debt. Often, this is at least sufficient to cover the down payment on the new property you're interested in. The interest paid on the loan may also be deductible from your taxes.

3. FHA Loans

The Federal Housing Administration offers a program to assist individuals in buying homes they plan to live in and is engaged in guaranteeing mortgages held by banks around the nation. Therefore, "investment property" is not, strictly speaking, covered by an FHA-backed loan. However, if you only reside in one of the units, the exemption clause enables you to utilize an FHA loan to purchase a house with up to four units. The key selling point of this kind of credit is the low down payment requirement of only 3.5%. However, if you put down less than 20%, you will need to purchase private mortgage insurance, which will slightly raise your monthly payments.

4. Hard money loans

A "hard money" loan is given out by a private company or investor as opposed to a bank with the aim of making a short-term investment. These loans might be hazardous, but they also provide investors the chance to sell or renovate profitable homes for a rapid return. Since hard money loans are often handled quickly, they also make it easier to purchase such properties before it's too late. Instead of considering collateral, the value of the property itself will be the primary factor in the decision to approve the loan. The time frame may be anything between six months and three years, and the interest rate is above average at 8% to 15%.

5. Portfolio loans

Unlike typical mortgages, portfolio loans are not resold to large banks like Fannie Mae and Freddie Mac on the secondary market. As a result, the lenders are not constrained to agree to the tight conditions established by the secondary buyer but rather are free to set whatever terms they are comfortable with. This may make portfolio loans more accessible to investors and self-employed borrowers than conventional mortgages. It's crucial to utilize recommendations, investor networks, and other resources to discover a lender since the majority of lenders who deal in portfolio loans don't promote their services. Otherwise, all you need to do is give each lender a call and specifically inquire as to whether they provide portfolio loans.

6. Commercial Loans

The other seven financing alternatives are mostly utilized for financing residential real estate, but business investments may also be quite alluring. A commercial loan will often have a shorter term and somewhat higher interest and fees. Another option that is often utilized for flipping commercial buildings is a company line of credit. With commercial loans, the revenue that the property is judged capable of producing is the primary approval criterion, as opposed to other loans where the borrower's income level is often the top consideration. Your financial background and track record in the commercial real estate investing sector will also be extensively examined.

7. 203K Loans

In many ways, a 203K loan is similar to an FHA loan. It varies, however, in that it enables you to borrow more funds to fund rehabilitation initiatives. Conveniently, this extra cash is already included in the principal real estate loan.

8. Private money loans

Although the lender and borrower have a deeper connection, these loans are quite similar to hard money loans. The ability to negotiate conditions that are agreeable to both parties is facilitated by this connection, and the interest rate, points, and fees are often substantially cheaper. However, if the borrower doesn't fulfill their responsibilities, the lender may still foreclose.

Chapter 6

Real Estate Exit Strategies

An Exit Strategy For A Business Is What?

An entrepreneur's plan to either sell or transfer ownership of a firm is known as an "exit strategy." An exit plan is, in essence, just what it sounds like: a way out. It may be used by business owners to increase profits or, if required, reduce losses. Before starting a company, entrepreneurs generally consider possible exit routes. This is due to the fact that exit strategies provide more than just a means of leaving a business. In the process, they also help to direct company choices.

When it comes to developing a company's exit strategy, there is no ideal solution. While some business owners may want to dissolve the company at a certain period, others may decide to sell shares to an existing partner. The best departure will depend on the size of the business and the owners' financial and timetable objectives, among other factors. It suffices to say that selecting the ideal company exit plan requires serious consideration. But when properly structured, it may act as a finish line and a motivation for company owners.

What Is An Exit Strategy For Real Estate?

Real estate exit strategies are plans that an investor uses to get out of a real estate transaction. Success depends on the choice to execute a strong exit plan since the right course of action will assure maximum rewards and the least dangers.

All too often, investors overlook how crucial it is to educate themselves on appropriate real estate exit alternatives. As a consequence, we have taken the opportunity to provide those who share our views a roadmap to a number of departure methods. This approach was designed with the intention of arming you with the knowledge required to make wise judgments when selecting the appropriate exit strategies for your agreements.

If investors shared this viewpoint, that would be excellent. Having an escape strategy is usually a wonderful idea, so you may leave safely if necessary! Investors that are cornered often don't have a backup plan, which might have a bad effect on them. But they could have spared a ton of time and short-term suffering if they had just concentrated on developing a plan of escape beforehand!

So many investors who had exit plans are now doing well or have done very well in this market.

4 Excellent Exit Strategies For Real Estate Investors

1. Promote the Home

Make sure there is a similar standard to other properties for sale in this neighborhood when seeking to sell quickly as an exit plan. This can include replacing that worn-out carpet right away or giving it a fast polish. Additionally, make an effort to sell the property somewhat below market value to increase the likelihood that it will sell quickly. The most common strategy used by investors may lead to profit quite rapidly (if the market is in excellent health)!

2. Vendor Financing

While you're exiting the market, property investment is a fantastic way to generate a return from your assets while you still choose to do so. This kind of financing often has a shorter term than other choices and a balloon payment.

When the seller serves as the bank to the person or people wishing to buy the property, this is known as "seller financing as an exit plan. The key distinction between this and a rent-to-own is that the buyer instantly has a beneficial ownership interest in the property. For instance, Bob may enter into a seller financing agreement as an alternative if his bank informs him that he is ineligible for a mortgage for any reason when he is trying to purchase a property. Bob's monthly payments are then collected by the property owner once they have agreed, taken their down payment, and financed the home under the predetermined conditions.

There are several sorts of seller financing. The aforementioned example would be a seller-financed mortgage. Land Contracts are another seller financing exit option for real estate investors.Essentially, this is when the buyer pays the seller on a regular basis for a certain amount of time until the last payment is made, at which point, and only at that point, do they obtain the entire legal title to the property.

- The advantage for the buyer

The fact that seller financing requires so little qualification is the key advantage for the buyer. The rules for obtaining a mortgage at a bank or mortgage broker are often more rigid than those used by the seller to assess the buyer's capacity to make timely payments. Additionally, there is flexibility when it comes to down payments since property owners sometimes let the buyer make smaller, more frequent installments as opposed to a single, quite substantial payment. Faster possession is another benefit, since purchasers and property owners won't have to wait as long for lenders to handle the financing of the transaction. Buyers often find this kind of property owner exit plan quite alluring!

- The advantages for the seller

The biggest advantage of using seller financing as an exit strategy for property owners is that they may demand the entire list price and perhaps even more since they are the ones providing the loan. Increased cash flow from the property is another huge advantage; it never hurts to have a little cash on hand! The seller may also qualify for significant tax benefits. Due to the fact that the transaction is being made in installments, the owner only has to disclose the revenue they get annually (spreading out their tax obligation), as opposed to the whole predicted profit all at once. The major benefit of seller financing is that it speeds up the sale of the property in a sluggish market. This is a terrific strategy to keep the market and your investment moving forward during times when people are struggling to buy houses!

3: Lease-purchase

A rent-to-own arrangement, commonly referred to as a lease option, enables the buyer to make larger monthly payments toward the home's purchase over a certain period of time. Due to the necessity to cover the cost of the down payment, these installments are higher than typical monthly payments. It is crucial to remember that just because purchasers consent to a rent-to-own agreement doesn't imply they have to buy the house at the conclusion of the agreement. If they decide to buy it in the end, it's up to them, but it's more like a long-term test drive!

- The advantage for the buyer

Continuous traveling may be physically and psychologically tiring, and it can also be expensive. Instead of wasting money on continual shifting, the major advantage of purchasing a rent-to-own is that buyers may take a "test drive" of the home and the neighborhood to see whether it is suited for them. Additionally, even if they don't have the best credit, buyers may still develop home equity via the asset! Finally, upon signing a contract, rent-to-own buyers have the option of holding onto their purchase price, which is quite advantageous if the location they are relocating to is appreciating rapidly.

- The advantages for the seller

A rent-to-own arrangement is a terrific way to sell your house someday and generate monthly income for yourself when the market is weak and homes are difficult to sell. Not everyone has the means to purchase a nice house, but that doesn't mean they wouldn't want to! This also implies that a renter who is a member of a rent-to-own arrangement will often be far better at preserving the home and their connections with their neighbors. Finally, since you're providing the renter a lot of freedom to decide whether or not to buy the property later, the regular monthly payment is often larger than it would be with rent.

4: Market and Flop

Everybody has seen HGTV and the incredible quick flips. For individuals who are just getting started in the market, it is undoubtedly a motivating interest. However, the biggest problem with this is that flips are harder than most people realize. As a means of exiting the real estate market, flipping homes entails purchasing a property that needs extensive repairs and improvements, updating it, and then selling it fast for more money than it was originally worth.

Investors frequently believe that adding extras like heated floors and automatic lights will persuade buyers to pay thousands more for their property, but the truth is that if the neighbors' property is on the market with significantly fewer upgrades but a lower asking price, the buyers will probably choose the neighbors. This is crucial to keep in mind if you're an investor who's considering flipping a home since, depending on the market, it could take a while to sell highly priced homes. Also, sometimes upgrades and fixes take longer than planned, which might cost you money since time is money!

Why Is It Important To Have An Exit Strategy?

An exit plan is crucial since it determines how investors will maximize profits while also guiding their actions throughout a particular transaction. Don't try to start a deal without considering possible escape alternatives, even if execution speed is crucial when facilitating a transaction. It is crucial for investors to analyze every circumstance with the eventual result in mind. Have a clear plan in mind before you buy each home, in other words. Before even meeting with a potential seller, investors should have a clear understanding of how they aim to earn from each real estate purchase.

Knowing each real estate exit option through and out may save your company hundreds, if not millions, of dollars over the course of a lifetime. Never bargain with a vendor if you don't know how you're getting out of the transaction. In addition to raising dangers, blind ambition will kill any opportunity of negotiating from a position of strength. Fundamentally, failing to plan an exit strategy decreases possible earnings while increasing risks.

Mistakes to Avoid With Real Estate Exit Strategies

Real estate investment is a reliable way to generate large sums of money and live the lifestyle you choose, but there are hazards that every investor has to be aware of. In particular, a planned real estate exit strategy may be hampered or even destroyed by a number of issues.

Any conceivable real estate escape options might be destroyed by the following elements:

- Tenant problems lead to a loss of rent.

A property may not be flipped due to a glaring lack of demand, a botched escrow, or a lender bailing out.

- Unexpected maintenance expenditures might negate any gains.
- Ineffective property management may reduce value and affect future cash flow.

- Deduction

Any investor must comprehend the reasons that might make the majority of real estate exit plans unsuccessful. Smart investors, however, use a variety of tactics to overcome possible difficulties. Since anything may change at any time, having a backup plan is essential. Having many real estate exit alternatives can help investors minimize potential risks and maximize their return on investment.

Investors who are still relatively new to the sector should stick to projects that have exit methods they are familiar with because of their lack of expertise. Always begin with ventures that need the least amount of labor for new investors. With more expertise, they may start taking on bigger projects that call for more intricate exit plans that might also be more lucrative.

But until then, it's always a good idea to be aware that you may always progress to the more sophisticated techniques after you've gained some expertise. By using this approach, you'll be placing yourself in the best possible position.

Chapter 7

Advice for a New Investor

5 Tips For New Investors Who Want To Make Money With Real Estate

Given that particular subtleties might mean the difference between a high-return investment and an average investor, it can be quite tempting to neglect them. The five elements covered in this essay may seem too basic at first, but they are the fundamentals you need to be aware of to get started under the appropriate circumstances. When you begin investing in real estate, don't make the error of ignoring these suggestions.

1. Describe your approach.

The foundation of any project is your strategy. When you have a good plan in place, you can remain on track, accomplish your goals, and avoid overextending yourself. This phase is crucial because you must ask yourself the correct questions and be well prepared in advance to effectively complete your investment project. When investing in real estate, you often make a long-term commitment if you use a bank or other financing institution. Therefore, it is essential to weigh all the risks and choose a method that works for you. An effective strategy must be built from a strong understanding of the industry. It is crucial to get training in the area to hasten the procedure.

2. Establish a budget.
Setting a budget in advance and sticking to it is crucial in this sector. Real estate is a fairly broad industry that benefits from being affordable for most budgets. If money is tight, you may start with a parking spot, a basement, or even a modest apartment. Your options will expand as your budget does. To avoid overstretching yourself, you should make your decision under your approach.

A rental property is still the greatest investment to make if, for instance, you wish to enhance your assets to become an annuitant and earn a livelihood from real estate. There are several choices: In addition to typical rentals, you may use seasonal rentals, home or apartment sharing, or other rental arrangements to boost your revenue flow. Profiting from resale after remodeling is another option. As you can see, there are several options, but your choice will ultimately depend on your approach.

3. Create a team
You are aware that buying a home requires help. To discover the rare pearl, you will need to collaborate with several individuals. Building a team that can assist you in acquiring your home in the best circumstances is crucial. You have a choice of using bailiffs, sellers, or real estate agents in your quest for your property (some bailiffs have access to a list of properties for sale). You will need to work with a notary as well as a bank or financing company to finance your property.

You will require a chartered accountant or a tax lawyer to determine your tax regime and calculate your profitability. You will need to deal with a contractor, a plumber, an electrician, and artisans for refurbishment and other projects. You have the option of doing rental management yourself, but if you don't want to, you may assign the task to another company. If this is your first investment, hiring a coach to work with you on your project might be of great assistance in making sure everything goes well.

4. purchase to generate money right now. You must set aside all of your emotions while making a real estate investment. People often overlook the fact that the agreement is formed at the time of purchase, not at the time of resale. They take action based on an emotional desire for something rather than a reasoned judgment, which results in the acquisition of a property at a price that is often greater than the market value.

They often believe that it makes no difference when purchasing this kind of property since they will sell it for twice as much five years from now. But no one can predict what will occur in five years. However, we can be certain that a high purchasing cost will have an impact on your project's profitability. Additionally, it is suggested that you bargain (within reasonable limits, of course). Remember that the first asking price made by a vendor is often too high since it allows for haggling.

5. Be persistent and patient while you seek
You need to be patient. It might take some time to find a property that fits your needs. Rushing into the first property you view, even if the cost is too high and the property does not suit your plan, is one of the worst blunders rookie investors make. Some individuals ultimately quit since they can't find a property that is lucrative enough. Expanding your assets will take time in the same manner. Contrary to what the media and success stories portray, money is not

built instantly; it takes time. And to do that, you'll need to stick to a well-laid-out plan.

Conclusion

The Future of Real Estate Investing

What Does Real Estate Investing Look Like in the Future?

As is well known, one of the most favored sectors of the global economy is real estate. The breadth of the real estate industry is expanding in terms of interest from more individuals. The company has a promising future because of how quickly the population is expanding. There is a greater demand for housing as the population grows.

Prices increase as a result of everything being in short supply and rising demand. On the one hand, this is why many now invest in real estate. On the other hand, they are drawn to developing brand-new, opulent-looking homes. People consider upgrading their existing homes or building new ones to mimic the look of wealthy homes while observing the opulent ones.

Has the real estate industry a future?

As we've already said, the real estate industry is expanding day and night. Because of this, the industry's future is quite promising. As more and more people move into urban areas to reside, contemporary amenities are becoming more important to today's population. Numerous stores are currently operational, and many more are being built, as can be seen.

With the conveniences just outside their homes, people are finding life to be more comfortable. They look for a property for sale in the neighborhood where everything is accessible because of this. Because of the public's mindset, developers decided to create housing societies. These housing associations stand for quality. Additionally, it has greatly improved the real estate industry's future.

Is Investing in Real Estate a Good Career?

Real estate is tied to almost 200 enterprises. Many individuals work in this industry, from creating a brick in a brick kiln to constructing a luxury home and multi-story retail center. Additionally, every person learns differently. A laborer makes less money than a developer, for instance. Among all of these stages and divisions, developers make the most money.

They purchase the property, develop it, and then sell the plots or homes, which is the rationale for this. Additionally, if you work hard as a real estate agent, you may make a respectable income.

Is investing in real estate the safest option?

Yes, from a variety of perspectives, real estate is among the safest investments. On the one hand, you could feel at ease knowing that your finances are safe. Additionally, you are free to use the property in any way you see fit.

Additionally, we advise investing in real estate if you want to make money without putting in any additional work. Additionally, if you need a second home, you may buy a property for sale to rent it out. With minimal effort, you may generate prospective income with minimal effort.

With this wonderful thing we call life, I wish you an enormous fortune and a lot of happiness.

www.ingramcontent.com/pod-product-compliance
Lightning Source LLC
LaVergne TN
LVHW050318160826
845677LV00014B/3467

* 9 7 9 8 8 4 7 4 1 4 4 2 5 *